Mel Bay Presents

KILLER-FILLERS

DRUM SET EXERCISES FOR TODAY'S DRUMMER

By James Morton

1 2 3 4 5 6 7 8 9 0

Visit us on the Web at www.melbay.com — E-mail us at email@melbay.com

INTRODUCTION

TYPES OF COORDINATION

When one moves from playing the snare drum to playing the drum set, three additional types of coordination come into play. Whereas, in snare drumming one is concerned primarily with hand-to-hand coordination (how one hand relates to the other in applying various rhythms, dynamics, and stickings), now, hand-and-foot coordination, independence and spatial coordination, must be considered. Hand-and-foot coordination is basically how one limb relates to the other three, and how they all relate to each other at the same time.

Hand-to-Hand Coordination:

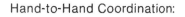

Hand-to-Foot Coordination

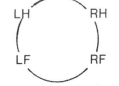

Independence is traditionally described as the ability to execute two or more counter-rhythms with either hands or feet. Regarding hand-to-hand coordination, hand-and-foot coordination, and independence, there are many fine instructional books one can study to sharpen these particular skills.

Spatial coordination can be defined as a discernment of the distance relationship of the drums and cymbals to each other and how one applies the three other types of coordination to that relationship. This concept is similar in nature to the way a mallet player must discern the distance between notes as he plays them. Developing spatial coordination is one of the aims of this book.

WHAT IS A FILL?

A fill is a rhythmic figure the drummer plays as sort of a departure from the time-keeping pattern he had been maintaining. Although it is a small break in the pattern, the tempo is not changed at all, and in most instances the time-keeping pattern is resumed immediately after the fill. Fills can vary as to style, length, and dynamics. A fill can be as subtle as a light touch with the brush on the cymbal or as forceful as a barrage of rolls around the drums. An important point to remember is that the flow of the music should not be sacrificed to the technicality of the fill. Actually, most fills are both simple in structure and short in duration. An attentive review of a broad spectrum of recordings will bear this out.

HOW FILLS ARE USED

Fills are utilized for a variety of functions, the simplest function being that they provide a break in the pattern being played. This break usually comes at the end of a 4, 8, 12, 16, or 32 bar phrase or section. Fills can also be transitional in nature. At the point where one section of a composition runs into another (verse to a chorus, verse to bridge, chorus to instrumental solo, etc.), a fill can be a useful pivotal point. Because fills can be a point of transition, they can also be considered musical "cues" to the listener that something new or different is coming up. This is especially effective when the change is dramatic (from a quiet passage to a very strong chorus, for example). Finally, a fill can be used to embellish a rhythm the band is emphasizing. If the band is punching this figure:

The drummer could punch the figure exactly as it is, or he could embellish it, perhaps like this:

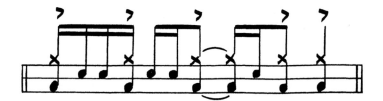

It is apparent that the tasteful and conservative use of fills can greatly enhance the drummer's contribution to the total ensemble sound. The exercises in this book are not meant to have direct application in playing situations. Rather they are intended to sharpen the drummer's spatial coordination skills and to give him enough accumulative experience to formulate his own fills in his own style.

HOW TO USE THIS BOOK

A three line staff relating to the basic setup of the snare drum, tom-tom, and floor tom, is used throughout the book:

High Tom⎯⎯⎯⎯⎯⎯⎯

Snare ⎯⎯⎯⎯⎯⎯⎯

Floor Tom⎯⎯⎯⎯⎯⎯⎯

All the exercises in this book are one measure fills in 4/4 time. Each exercise should be played as a fill between time-keeping patterns. The following are three examples of time-keeping patterns with a straight eighth note or sixteenth note feel:

I suggest that as a way of practice you play three measures of time, play the one measure exercise, and then return to playing time. Play three more measures of time and then the second exercise, and so on. By following this pattern, you are playing a fill every fourth measure.

Example:

REPEAT EACH EXERCISE YOU ARE NOT SURE OF.

MAKE EACH NOTE CLEAN AND DEFINITE.

WHILE PLAYING THE FILLS IT IS SUGGESTED THAT YOU KEEP TIME (QUARTER NOTES) ON THE BASS DRUM.

PRACTICE HARD AND GOOD LUCK.

SINGLE STROKE 16TH NOTES

Aug. 15 21 - 30

Aug. 22

31 - 40

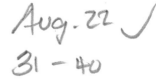

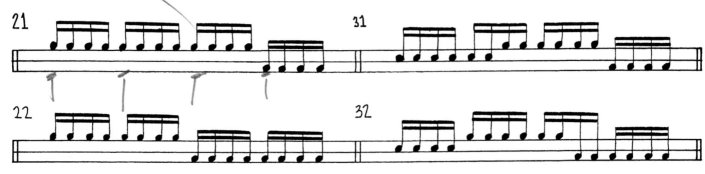

41  51

42

43

44

45

46

47

48

49

50

Aug. 8
61-70 ✓

USE METRONOME
mm = 80

81  91

82  92

83  93

84  94

85  95

86  96

87  97

88  98

89  99

90  100

11

121

122

123

124

125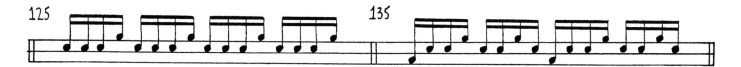

126

127

128

129

130

12

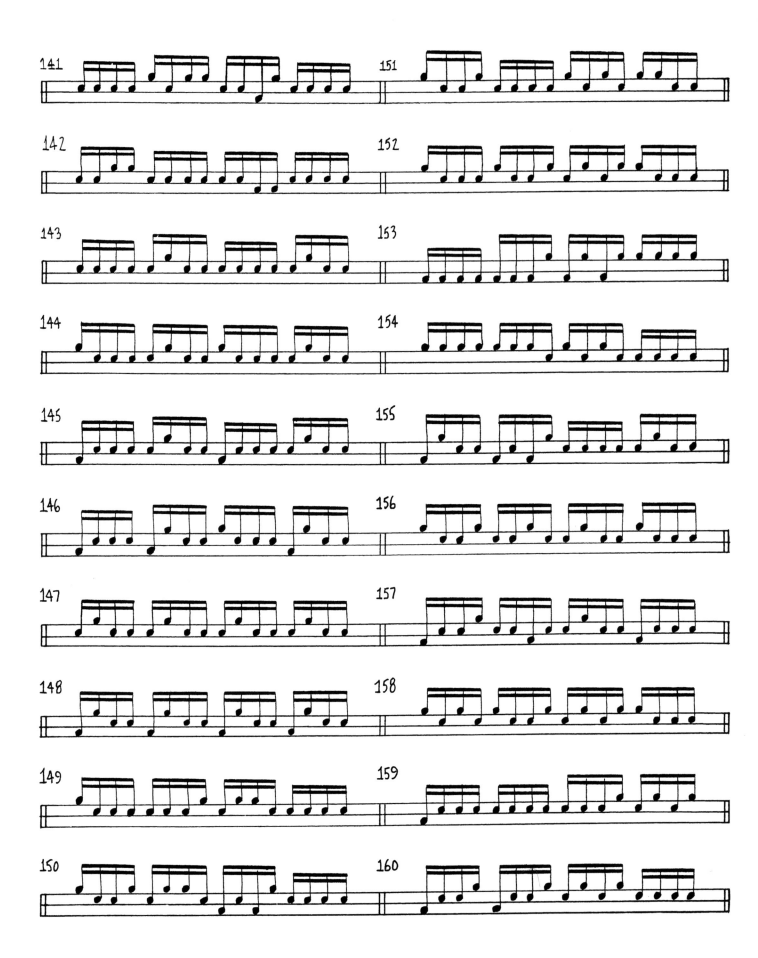

SINGLE STROKE 16TH NOTE TRIPLETS

14

15

16

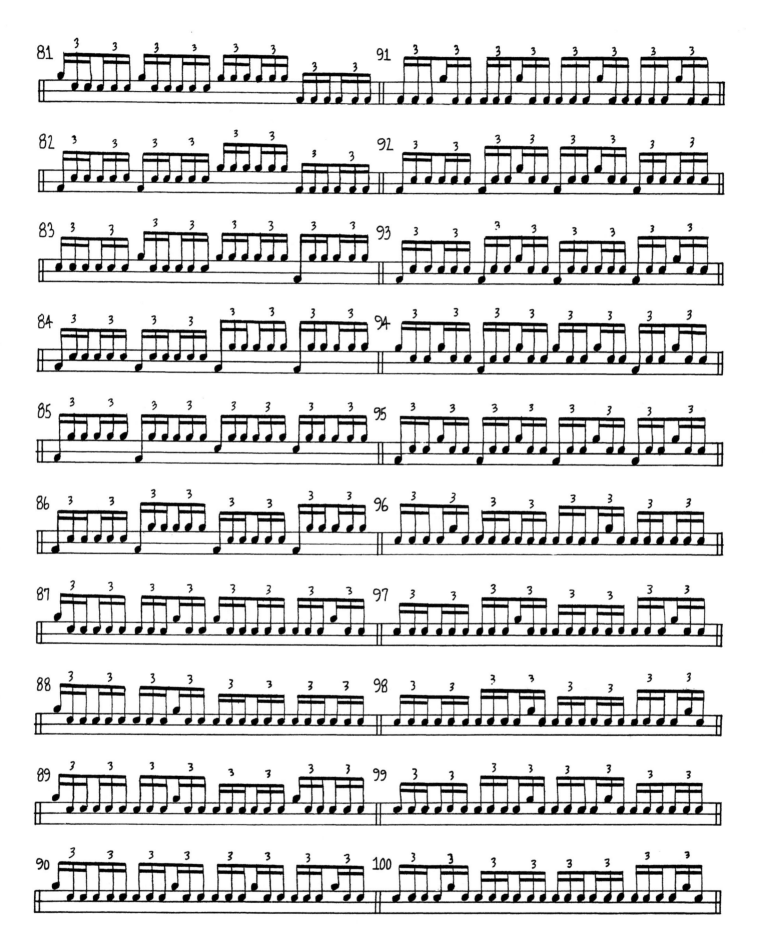

18

SINGLE STROKE 32ND NOTES

DOUBLE STROKE 32ND NOTES

24

41  51

42  52

43  53

44  54

45  55

46  56

47  57

48  58

49  59

50 60

61  71

62  72

63  73

64  74

65 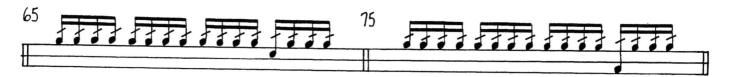 75

66  76

67  77

68  78

69  79

70  80

26

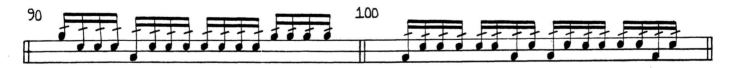

101

111

102

112

103

113

104

114

105

115

106

116

107

117

108

118

109

119

110

120

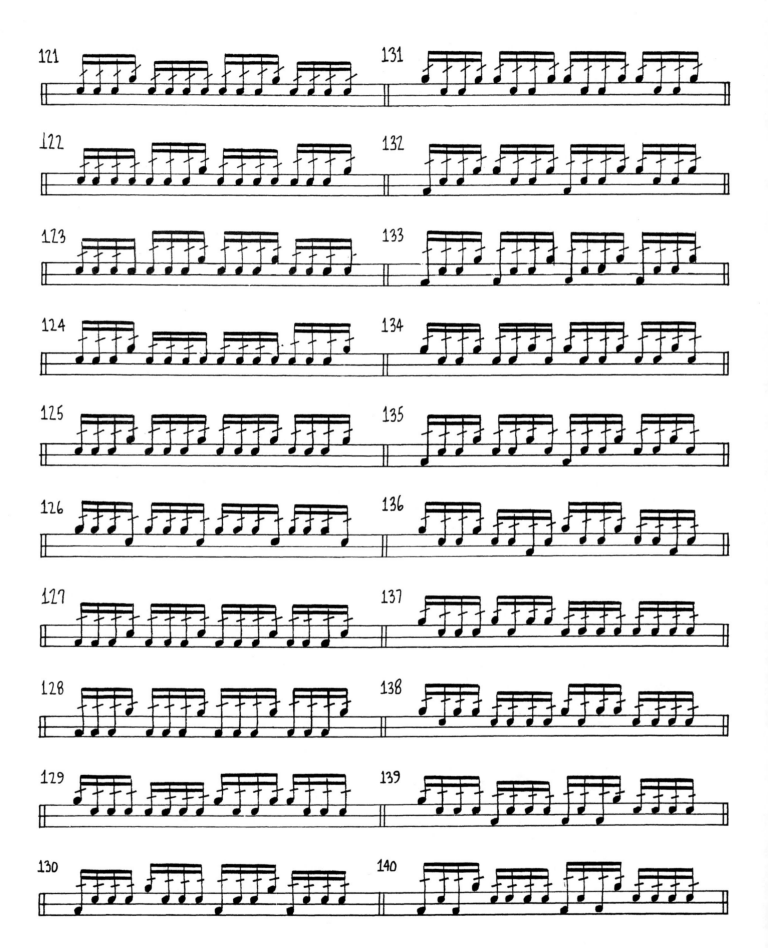

141

151

142

152

143

153

144

154

145

155

146

156

147

157

148

158

149

159

150

160

21

31

22

32

23

33

24

34

25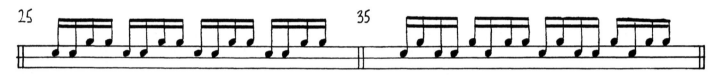

35

26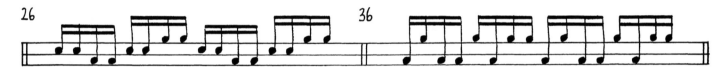

36

27

37

28

38

29

39

30

40

SIMULTANEOUS STICKING

*Exercises 1-4 are based on the Flam Paradiddle; # 5-11 are based on the Flam Accent; # 12-15 are based on the Flamacue. Although based on flam rudiments, these exercises are meant to be played with simultaneous stickings, and not with grace notes.

34

*This exercise to be played with a one hand crush roll.

*For # 10 use one hand buzz roll.   *For # 11 & 12 'x' = rim shot.

FILLS USING BASS DRUM AND HI-HAT

1
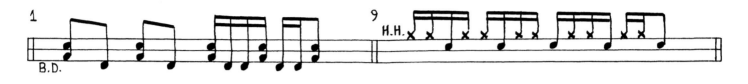
B.D.

9
H.H.

2
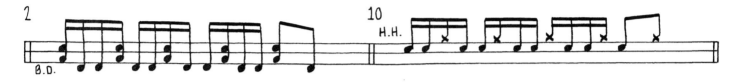
B.D.

10
H.H.

3
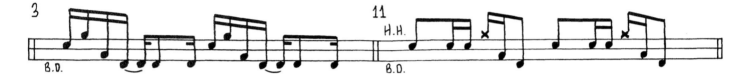
B.D.

11
H.H.
B.D.

4
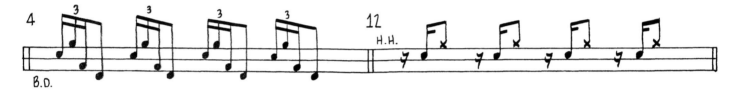
B.D.

12
H.H.

5
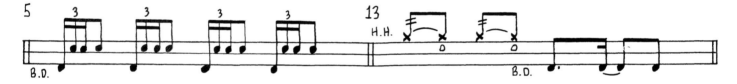
B.D.

13
H.H.
B.D.

6
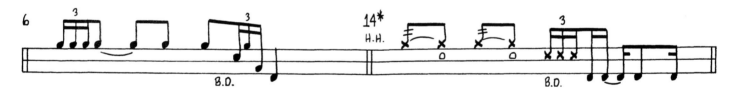
B.D.

14*
H.H.
B.D.

7
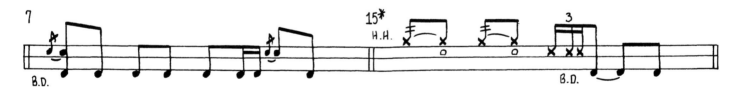
B.D.

15*
H.H.
B.D.

8
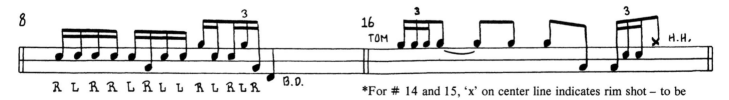
R L R R L R L L L R L R L R   B.D.

16
TOM
H.H.

*For # 14 and 15, 'x' on center line indicates rim shot – to be

played one stick rapping the other on drum.

There are several styles of music that share the same time signature. Dynamics, tempo, rhythm construction, and accentuation are among the factors which determine which style of music is being played. Nearly all swing, blues, shuffle music, and much of jazz, hard rock and ballads are either in 12/8 time or in 4/4 time with a triplet feel. This final section of the book concerns triplet fills that can accommodate the following rhythm patterns. These are just a few examples of an infinite number of possibilities:

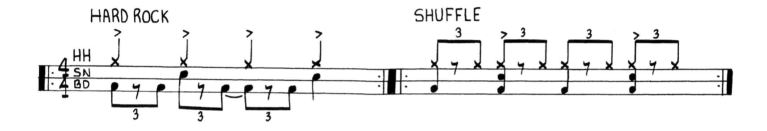

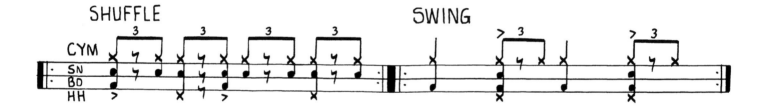

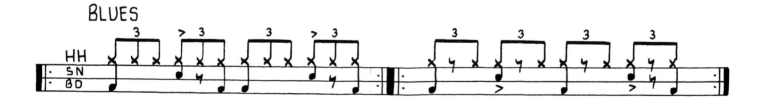

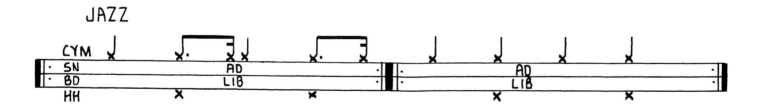

*Hi-Hat Notation:
  o = played open with stick
  + = played closed with stick
  − = not struck but closed with foot.

Great Music at Your Fingertips